The Let's Talk Library™

Let's Talk About Feeling Confused

Melanie Ann Apel

The Rosen Publishing Group's

PowerKids Press™

New York

For Mom, Dad, and Mindy, my wonderful family. With all my love, Melanie.

Published in 2001 by The Rosen Publishing Group, Inc.
29 East 21st Street, New York, NY 10010

First Edition

Book Design: Maria Melendez

Photo Credits: pp. 4, 7, 8, 11, 15, 16, 19, 20 by Myles Pinkney; p. 12 © Skjold Photography.

Apel, Melanie Ann.
    Let's talk about feeling confused / by Melanie Ann Apel.
      p. cm.— (Let's talk about library)
    Includes index.
    Summary: This book discusses what it means to be confused and things that can be done to avoid being confused.
    ISBN 0-8239-5623-7
    1. Human information processing in children—Juvenile literature. [1. Thought and thinking.
2. Decision making.] I. Title. II. Series.

BF723.T63 A64 2000
155.4—dc21   00-036711

Manufactured in the United States of America

Contents

George and Jamal

George and Jamal have been best friends for two years. George thinks Jamal is the nicest kid he knows. Then a new boy named Peter starts coming to their school. Jamal and Peter do not get along. They say mean things to each other. George is surprised by how nasty Jamal acts toward Peter. George cannot believe that his best friend can be so mean. George wonders whether Jamal is a good friend to have. George is confused.

◀ *When your friend acts in a way that you are not used to, it can be very confusing.*

What Does It Mean to Be Confused?

When you are confused, it means that you are not sure about something. You may not understand what a teacher or your parent is saying to you. You may be having a hard time making a **decision** because you are not sure what to do about a problem. You can also get confused when something turns out differently than you thought. Maybe you thought your friend would be happy when you brought your neighbor over to play. If your friend becomes angry instead, you might be confused.

People don't always act the way you think they will. This can make you feel confused. ▶

Who Gets Confused?

Everyone gets confused! Kids get confused and so do grown-ups. It is normal to feel unsure about things sometimes. Grown-ups do not always explain things in a way that you can understand. This can make you feel confused. You might see something on television that confuses you. You might not understand some of the words being used on the television show. You might not be able to follow the story. Learning new things can be confusing. Just remember that as you learn more you will understand more. Then you will feel a lot less confused.

◀ *Try not to get upset if you don't understand something right away. With patience and practice, things will seem much less confusing.*

The Rules of the Game

Jay and Kelly just got a new game. Kelly reads the rules. She has trouble understanding them. She thinks they are confusing. Jay takes a turn reading the rules. He reads them very carefully. When he thinks he understands the rules, he reads them out loud. He explains the rules to Kelly in his own words. Jay helps Kelly understand the rules of the game. Kelly is not confused anymore.

If you don't understand the rules of a game, ask your friend for help. That way you both will have more fun! ▶

Are You Confused?

If you get confused, try not to get upset about it. If you never got confused, that would probably mean you never tried anything new. It can be hard to remember things as you are learning. You may think you remember how to do something. Then you find out that you have made a mistake. This can make you feel confused. Do not forget that this will get better with time and practice. Feeling confused about making a decision can be a good thing. It means you are thinking carefully about your decision and trying to make the right choice.

◀ *If you feel confused when making a decision, it means you are taking your life and your choices seriously. Don't worry too much, though. Just do the best you can.*

What to Do When You Are Confused

If something is confusing you, you might not know what to do. The best way to figure out what to do is by speaking up. Don't be shy. Explain to a grown-up that you are confused. Let them know that you need things explained in a different way. When you think you understand, check to make sure that you are right. Repeat what you have been told. Ask if you have understood correctly.

Grown-ups are happy to help you when you are confused. Never be afraid to speak up. Everyone gets confused at times. ▶

Getting Lost

Michelle and Luke walked to the park. While they were there, they played with their dogs. One of the dogs ran out of the park. Luke went after the dog. He ended up in an **unfamiliar** neighborhood. Luke was confused. He didn't know how to get back to Michelle. Luke started calling Michelle's name. Michelle had seen which way Luke had gone. She caught up with him. Getting lost is another **experience** that can make you feel confused. It is easy to **panic** if you get lost. Try to stay calm, though. This will help you think more clearly.

◄ *Try not to panic if you get lost. When you are calm, you can think more clearly. This will help you find your way home.*

How to Avoid Being Confused

Sometimes there are things you can do to avoid being confused. When your teacher is explaining something new, listen carefully to what he or she is saying. Pay attention the whole time. That way, you are more likely to understand. When you are reading a chapter in a book for homework, you might get confused as to what the chapter is about. Don't forget to read carefully and slowly. If you do these things, you will understand what you are reading better. Paying attention to what you are doing can help you avoid being confused.

The more carefully you read something, the more you will understand. This is a great way to avoid being confused. ▶

Sarah's Big Decision

Sarah loves baseball. It is her favorite sport. As a surprise, her father buys tickets for the opening game of her home team. Sarah cannot wait to go. The next day she gets an invitation to her friend's birthday party. The party and the baseball game are on the same day. Sarah has a big decision to make. She wants to go to both the party and the baseball game. She has to pick one or the other, though. Sarah is confused about what to do.

Choosing between two things you love can get very confusing.
◀ *Make the best choice you can. There will always be time to do the things you love most.*

It's Okay to Feel Confused

As you grow and learn more, you will become less confused. You will also learn how to decide which things are the most important to you. This will help you be sure about decisions you need to make. There will still be times when you get confused, though. This happens to everyone. Do the best you can and move on. The most important thing is to learn from your experiences. Something that might be confusing the first time it happens will be easier to deal with the next time. You will have learned a lot, too. This is what makes life so interesting!

Glossary

decision (di-SIZH-un) A choice a person makes about something.

experience (ik-SPIR-ee-ents) Knowledge or skill gained by doing or seeing something.

panic (PA-nik) An uncontrolled feeling of fear.

unfamiliar (un-fuh-MIL-yur) Strange, not known.

Index